Wonderfully Free... no going back!

A 31-day devotional journal to follow up your Sozo

First printed 2019

For all further details contact darrellcocup@gmail.com.

ISBN- 978-164440580-2

Cover design and typesetting by Chris Pink www.chrispink.co.uk
USA editing by Angie Carnes Sinclair

Let me be clear, the Anointed One has set us free – not partially, but completely and wonderfully free! We must always cherish this truth and stubbornly refuse to go back to the bondage of our past.
GALATIANS 5:1
THE PASSION TRANSLATION

To Anthea, who deserves far more dedication than this

Thanks

To the following wonderful people who, in adding a piece of themselves, have made this possible:

For Early Guidance: Alan and Jan Kilpatrick, Ruth Senior, and Chris Wright.

To my fellow Bath City Church Life Group colleagues: Sue Dakin for steering the Prayer and Responses, Jackie Parker and Hillary Law for corrections, Robin Henderson for editing, correcting, typesetting, tidying and encouragement.

A big thanks also to our friends in the USA who commented on and made useful suggestions to this work, especially Laurie Westwood, Melissa Alvarez, and Robert Muncy,

you're all great!

To Dawna and Teresa, without whom...

Contents

Kind Words!

Confidentiality is vital with Sozo. I've honored this by not showing the name of the Sozo guests who agreed to "trial" this journal following their Sozo, and who fed back their comments.

"A great piece of work! I just imagine you in the room chatting through the content. It's easy to read and very accessible.

It seems to be the accumulated wisdom you have picked up over the years of doing Sozo. Essential reading for Sozo practitioners as well as guests, I reckon."
Sozo Guest

"I think this is absolutely brilliant. You have done a fantastic job putting it together. You've done a lot of work, and I think it is a definite asset to the Sozo ministry. Many people have a hard time remembering what went on in their Sozo, and this helps them to recall things that Holy Spirit revealed and to also keep short accounts with the Godhead. When things come up, they can deal with them right away. It would be great to give to each person after their session to help them walk out what they have received. Great job."
Susan Rashotte
Sozo Facilitator, Canada

"I want to comment on Wonderfully Free.
When I heard about this project, I was very excited. When I am teaching and doing Sozos, there is always the question, "What's next?" My advice is always to use what they have experienced and continue the conversation that began in the session with the Godhead.
I always suggest this, but there is a feeling that they could use a bit more help.

After reading Wonderfully Free, I was glad that help has arrived. This book is exactly the vehicle needed to help people continue in their freedom. I believe it will solidify the truths that were spoken so that they can be walked out more quickly. I feel it will help us have fewer repeat sessions. It will be able to help the client move on to the next place that Papa wants them to go.

It will be amazing to have this resource for people that want to accelerate what happened in their Sozo. I will want to have many copies available on hand."
Laurie Westwood
Sozo Facilitator, Delaware, New Jersey, New York, and Pennsylvania

"What I believe Sozo is about is not only offering individual sessions but promoting a mindset of freedom and being open to know our true selves, warts and all so that God can reveal where we have need for healing. We need ongoing healing – you could call it the process of redemption – that is a given – but perhaps few realize this or know how to pursue it.

Whereas one Sozo session alone can be transforming, what we really want to do is set people on the path of traveling further and further in the journey and lifestyle of that healing - you could also say it in terms of our minds being renewed. Sozo is a way of thinking, not just a visit to the operating table.

Wonderfully Free seems to fill a gap that has existed in that respect. Going over truths after a Sozo is good, but an encouragement to do that and go further down the road is better. Wonderfully Free both reinforces the Sozo and points ahead to the possibility of further truths being encountered."
SOZO GUEST

"I have really enjoyed working through this devotional. I have not always been able to do it each day, and there was a gap when I was away for a week. However, although probably best done daily, I have gained much benefit from it, and I thought it was good your introduction gave permission if days were missed. This took away the pressure. A number of the areas covered in my Sozo cropped up in the early part of the devotional. It felt like the loose ends were tied up and closure was brought to some of the issues. I also found that on days when there were no particular issues, just dwelling with the Bible verses and processing the thoughts for that day was uplifting.

Wonderfully Free is well laid out; it continues the Sozo process in a structured way. It encourages spending time with God and hearing more truths and affirmations.

Thank you for inviting me to be a part of this exciting journey. I have found the devotional beneficial and enriching. I would recommend it to others."
SOZO GUEST

"I think your book is absolutely BRILLIANT!! How has someone not written it before now?! I love the Day 1 entry about getting to know a friend that you sing to or about on a Sunday, and then listen to someone talk about them. It is so simple and yet hugely profound. Also, I love the pastoral heart of God that comes through at the start of Day 3 on hearing, sensing, and feeling. Your words carry care and kindness, and that is sooo lovely!

As my last Sozo was a wee while ago, I asked God to highlight and remind me of what He wanted me to explore more from previous Sozo sessions through the book and that has been really affirming to see how far that I've come.

Thank you!"
SOZO GUEST

Introduction

Bethel Sozo is sometimes described as being a healing and deliverance ministry, but as you'll have discovered, it's so much more than that! Bethel Sozo's leading task is to help you to have a personal relationship with Father God, Jesus, and Holy Spirit – a relationship in which you are either reminded or learn how to hear, see, sense, or feel God as He reaches out relentlessly in pursuit of you, His beloved.

It's up to you how to respond to His call. As you uncover, face, and deal with the wounds and lies that have held you personally back from becoming all that He has made you to be, you will experience the clear, clean water of His love and truth washing away the murky blackness of the past, whatever that held for you.

Each new day offers another opportunity to make it different from the one before, and that's really what this journal is about. In your Sozo, you may have recognized that some of your thinking and life choices need to change so there's more room for His love and truth to fill you and for your relationship with God to go deeper ... and now it's a new day and the first days of the rest of your life. Is it time for those changes and to make more room?

The answer, as mentioned above, is that it's entirely up to you. It's your choice whether you go back to believing what you did before your Sozo or, instead, to believe the truths you heard during it. This journal aims to help you with that.

For each of the next 31 days we'll be looking at a different aspect of the Sozo enriched life and seeing what the Bible says about it.

For each day, we've chosen a few short extracts and would encourage you to read these verses in different versions of the Bible to see which impacts you the most. If you want to do this online, you could use www.biblehub.com, but there are lots to choose from. We've chosen from the Passion Translation but left room for you to add others.

We've found that the very act of writing out the Word brings it closer and makes it more personal and memorable. You may also want to use some of these Scriptures as declarations (see Day 5).

- Prayer and Response – We'll be making suggestions every day, but the way you respond is entirely up to you. We recommend that as you begin to hear, see, sense, and feel in response to the morning's readings and prayer time, you journal it. We talk about this on Day 4, but we suggest that you start journaling on Day 1! You don't have to do it here, but there's space in case you want to keep a record of your progress and thoughts in one place. We recommend you do!

Important! It's more important for you to get as much as you can from each exercise than it is for you to keep up to date. What really matters is that you bring the truths of your Sozo into your everyday life, no matter how long it takes! So...

- Give yourself permission to fall behind. If, for example, you have a busy day or you're traveling, or for whatever reason, you don't have enough time, then take the day off. If this happens, don't try and catch up in a rush because completing each day properly will be of more benefit than keeping up to date.

- If you find that some days require some extra time to process, then take an extra day (or more) to do this.

- You may decide to space your journey over a couple of months or more (or less).

- To help you keep on track and to help with your journaling, we've left space at the start of each exercise for the date.

But Before You Start…

How much of your Sozo do you remember? In fact, why did you apply for one in the first place? If you're going to take this 31- Day journey, it's probably a good idea to begin at the beginning so that your story is complete. What follows are a few questions to get you going, but don't stop with these. Journal what you remember of what took place and how it made you feel.

What made you decide to apply for a Sozo?

How were you feeling on the days leading up to your Sozo?

What did you think was going to happen?

How did you feel as God started to speak into your life?

What do you feel God did for you during your Sozo?

Were you left with any questions?

How do you feel heading into the next 31 days?

The next morning, Jesus got up long before daylight, left the house while it was dark, and made his way to a secluded place to give himself to prayer.

MARK 1:35 TPT

Date

Spending Time with the Godhead

How easy is it to build a friendship with someone you never spend time with or talk to? It's not really possible, is it? Let's put it another way. If you had a friend who you visited every Sunday morning, who you spent some time singing songs to or about, you listened to someone talking about your friend, and then you went home, how good would that be for developing your friendship? It wouldn't really be good at all, but that's what a lot of us of do with God. We just visit Him on a Sunday morning and don't work on building a real friendship.

Hopefully, your Sozo was different, and you were able to spend quality time speaking to and hearing from Father God, Jesus, and Holy Spirit, but don't worry if this was a struggle and didn't happen easily. Being able to discern the Voice-of-God in your head and to differentiate it from your other thoughts can be a challenge. In Sozo, we tell people to go with the very first thing they hear or sense or feel in response to the question they've asked because experience tells us that's God. If hearing, sensing, or feeling is a problem, have faith in the first thing that comes to you. The Good News is that once you know it's God, you can keep that conversation going wherever you are and whenever you want. There are not many friends who will spend their entire time chasing you to get your attention so that you include them in your life every day, but that's what God does – for one simple reason – He loves you deeply! So, why not make the decision today to build your friendship with Father God, with Holy Spirit, and with Jesus?

Reading:

> *The next morning, Jesus got up long before daylight, left the house while it was dark, and made his way to a secluded place to give himself to prayer.*
> MARK 1:35 TPT

Also Read:

Colossians 4:2

Hebrews 10:22

Prayer and Response:

Father God, I don't want to spend my life having a distant relationship with You, Jesus, and Holy Spirit. Today, I choose to continue hearing and sensing You as I did in my Sozo. I choose to live close to You, be aware of You, and able to speak to and hear from You, knowing You in my every day. Please show me how to have the discipline to do what it takes to build "You time" into my life, to carve out a space for me to pray, to hear and to share my life with You – whatever that looks like. Amen.

Ask Father God what carving out a space looks like and how to implement this.

Be ready to hear, see, sense, or feel the same way as you did in your Sozo. Listen to God and see what He wants to say to you about getting closer. Expect to hear from Him with guidance.

He'll show you! Then write down what He says to you.

My own sheep will hear my voice and I know each one, and they will follow me.

John 10:27 TPT

Date

Hearing, Sensing, Seeing, and Feeling

We're spending another day on hearing, sensing, seeing, and feeling because it's so important! How do you hear from God? Do you have an audible voice in your head that you know to be Father God, Jesus, or Holy Spirit when you hear it, or do you just have an inner sense and know it is from God? Perhaps you see pictures that have meaning or maybe your feelings are stirred in ways that you know come from nowhere else, or perhaps, for you, it's a combination of all these.

Maybe, as we mentioned yesterday, none of these apply to you, and you feel that God doesn't want to or hardly ever talks to you. Perhaps you went through your Sozo answering the questions from your head without any notion of a Godly download. Do you know that can be okay? Let us explain:

If you haven't been used to listening to God, being asked to do so in your Sozo might have been a bit challenging. If it was something new for you, then you might well have expected something different to happen, an additional voice in your head or a new sense of something. This might have happened, or it may not have. The Bible talks about God's still small voice, but this can be difficult to discern amongst the background noise of everything else going on in your head. What's important to know is that God's voice is there. Once you've accepted Jesus into your life and Holy Spirit into your being, then you can live knowing that God is constantly reaching out to you. He'll do it through the Bible. He'll do it through your senses. He'll do it through your thoughts. He'll speak to you in your dreams. You're on a journey of discovery, of learning how to discern Him and then how to respond to what He tells and shows you.

Here's a suggestion in learning to listen: When you ask Father God, Holy Spirit, or Jesus a question, the very first thought, picture, or feeling you have, as we said yesterday, is probably God. Don't dismiss it. If it's in alignment with the Bible, then presume it is Him! As the relationship deepens, and over time, you'll learn to trust the origin of your thoughts and feelings more and more.

Reading:

> *My own sheep will hear my voice and I know each one, and they will follow me.*
> JOHN 10:27 TPT

Also Read:

Psalm 34:4-5

Prayer and Response:

In your own words, thank Father God for wanting to reach out and communicate with you. Tell Him how much you want to be able to hear, see, sense, and feel from Him. Tell Him how much that means to you and then see what He tells you. Be prepared to write down what you hear, see, sense, or feel.

Whatever you write down is just for you. It doesn't have to be "right." Don't try and sift what comes to you – just write it down. As you come to the end of your journaling, take a minute to ask Jesus whether there's anything else that He would like to tell you or that He feels you should know.

A dear friend will love you no matter what. And a family sticks together through all sorts of trouble.
Proverbs 17:17 TPT

Date

Sharing your Walk

You'll have completed an application form before having your Sozo. Most of these have on them a comment which reads something like this:

"Do you attend a life/cell/home group as part of your Church? If not, we recommend you join one. We suggest that you find an accountability partner with whom to share your Sozo experience and help you to walk out your Godly truths."

Why would we suggest that? Because life is all about relationships. Simply put, you were never meant to be on your own. People are designed to share, to live in community, to rely on others, and to be relied on by others. Life may have forced you into being a loner, but that's not God's plan for you. If that was an issue in your Sozo, we hope you now know the truth that God loves you and finds you utterly acceptable. Not only that, but somewhere close to you, there's a community of Christians, many of whom have shared many of the same experiences you have and all of whom are ready to welcome you into their midst. It may mean having to step out of your comfort zone, but it's important to find or choose someone with whom you can share your Sozo and who'll be able to help keep you on track and accountable, so you don't allow the lies of the past to re-establish themselves. You are bestowing a great honor when you ask someone to mentor you or keep you accountable. Don't hold back from giving that honor to someone.

Reading:

> *A dear friend will love you no matter what. And a family sticks together through all sorts of trouble.*
> PROVERBS 17:17 TPT

Also Read:

Proverbs 18:24

Proverbs 27:6

Proverbs 27:17

Prayer and Response:

Father God, thank You that You're the God of change and that, through You, all things are possible. Thank You for my Sozo and for showing me the lies that I've believed about myself all these years. Thank You for revealing to me the truth and for showing me how much You love me and how special I am to You. I choose to believe that truth and to make it mine. Thank You that I can see and do life knowing I'm a beloved son/daughter of the Most High. I can now see life through Your eyes and not through the lenses I've been wearing until now. I declare the truth that I am loved, and that life is going to be different from now on. Amen.

What's different since your Sozo? What has changed?

How does it feel to be different? Can you describe this difference in words? Try writing it down.

Ask Jesus who you should ask to be accountable to and what that should look like.

This is what the Lord, the God of Israel, says: Write down for the record everything I have said to you, Jeremiah.
Jeremiah 30:2 NLT

Date

Journaling

Over the last couple of days we've talked about the need to share your Sozo walk with other Christians and then to make sure you find the time to spend with Father God, Jesus, and Holy Spirit, developing your friendship with them.

How might you do that?

We read yesterday that one way God speaks to us is through His Word. When reading your Bible, a passage that you've seen many times will suddenly reach out from the page and grab your attention in a way it never has before. As you read it, you'll know in your spirit that God had that passage for you that day. But how else might you know?

We would suggest journaling. Keeping a diary and journaling are not the same. A diary is where you write and keep a record of the flow of your own impressions and thoughts on paper. Journaling, on the other hand, is more about writing down what you feel, see, and sense in response to the conversation you have with the Godhead. If you think about it, that's what you were doing during your Sozo. You were having a conversation with God and hearing from Him. All we're suggesting is that you continue the conversation in your quiet time and write down what comes to you. Over time, you'll hear, see, and feel more clearly. Also, what you've written down will begin to make real sense in your life. Try it. You'll be glad you did, especially when, in the future, you're able to look back and see what has changed for you.

Wonderfully Free… no going back!

Reading:

This is what the Lord, the God of Israel, says: Write down for the record everything I have said to you, Jeremiah.
Jeremiah 30:2 NLT

Also Read:

Psalm 119:27

Prayer and Response:

There are different ways to journal. You could try two-way journaling. This involves writing down your thoughts and feelings as if you were writing a letter to God. Once you've finished your "letter," stop and ask God to speak to you and write down what He says. Don't rush this. Like the other day, write it all down. You can then pray over it and discard what doesn't ring true.

So then, my soul, why would you be depressed? Why would you sink into despair? Just keep hoping and waiting on God your Savior. For no matter what, I will still sing with praise, For living before his face is my saving grace!
Psalm 42:5 TPT

Date

Declarations

During your Sozo, you will have broken and removed the right for many negative thought patterns and lies to rule in your life. Now, you have to learn to walk free of the residual habits that formed because of those lies. God will have revealed the truths which replace those lies. What you should do now is to build these new truths into your life by declaring them.

What does this look like? Of course, it depends what the lies were, but you'll recognize them the moment they crop up! For example, they could include: "When I look in the mirror, I'm ugly." "I can't drive on freeways." "I can't speak in public." … or "I'm not good enough for this." If God has told you that these are lies and revealed the truth to you, believe Him – He knows you better than you know yourself. To break the habit, you have to challenge the lie, and we suggest you do this by declaring truth.

Steve Backlund, one of the pastors at Bethel Church, writes and talks about the importance of making declarations. Declaring the truth of who you are as God sees you is much more powerful than just self-talk. It shifts atmosphere. It changes the spiritual environment. It gives notice to the enemy that the past is done and that God's Word rules. Declarations are powerful, and they're best done out loud! In Sozo, we believe that the enemy can't read your mind, but he can certainly hear your voice. So, don't hold back in your declarations!

Reading:

So then, my soul, why would you be depressed? Why would you sink into despair? Just keep hoping and waiting on God your Savior. For no matter what, I will still sing with praise, For living before his face is my saving grace!
PSALM 42:5 TPT

Also Read:

Galatians 2:20

Prayer and Response:

Today, make your response your prayer too! Turn all the truths that you received in your Sozo into declarations and prayers. Write them down. Then declare them out loud over yourself for at least the next 30 days. What does this look like? Well, if Father God has told you that He finds you clever and beautiful and He loves you, then speak it out! "I declare that I am a beautiful daughter/son of God. I declare that I'm clever. I declare that I'm loveable and that He loves me!" If that's what you've heard, that's the truth. Who are you or anyone else to think otherwise?

Look with wonder at the depth of the Father's marvelous love that he has lavished on us! He has called us and made us his very own beloved children. The reason the world doesn't recognize who we are is that they didn't recognize him.

1 JOHN 3:1 TPT

Date

The Role of Father God

In Sozo, we recognize that, ideally, a dad's role in our lives should be to protect us, provide for us, and help us to grow up knowing our identity. The trouble is, this isn't always our experience. How easy was it in your Sozo to deal with the forgiveness issues around your Dad? Was there lots to do or is/was your Dad an all-round good guy who showered you with love? Occasionally people come for a Sozo and have absolutely nothing they feel the need to forgive their dads for, but that's a rarity. More often than not, a lot of someone's first Sozo is spent thinking about and forgiving their Dad.

What's important to recognize is that forgiving your Dad doesn't necessarily mean you are dishonoring him. He might, for example, have been serving in the armed forces on the other side of the world, which in itself was fine, but he wasn't there for you growing up. He wasn't there when you needed him, and forgiveness is needed for the pain of his absence and the feelings of abandonment that might have followed.

Unintentionally, we often assign to Father God the same attributes, or lack of them, as our own Dads have or had. In the above example of the dad serving in the armed forces, it's easy to start to think that Father God could abandon us too or that He's not interested enough to be there for us when we need Him. We tend to place our Dad's face onto the face of Father God, thinking He'll be exactly like our Dad, and the truth is – He's not!

Hopefully, your Sozo helped you to understand this, and you now have a much better relationship with Father God than you had before. Now's the time to develop that relationship, to share the ups and downs of your life with Him, and to get His input. You'll know His voice because it will sound the same as it did in your Sozo!

Reading:

> *Look with wonder at the depth of the Father's marvelous love that he has lavished on us! He has called us and made us his very own beloved children. The reason the world doesn't recognize who we are is that they didn't recognize him.*
>
> 1 John 3:1 TPT

Also Read:

John 14:7–11

Prayer and Response:

> *Father God, I thank You for showing me that You are a good Father and that Your love for me has no bounds and no boundaries. I know that whatever I've done – I'm forgiven, and that whatever I do – You'll forgive me if I turn to You in true repentance. I know I can trust You with my innermost thoughts and my most outrageous dreams. I know that You want me to know Your protection and be secure in being Yours. I choose, Father God, to learn how to become the person You made me to be so that I know not just who I am but Whose I am. Amen.*
>
> *You can't make yourself feel loved, but you can begin to love yourself. Your Sozo will have revealed the lies you've been believing about Father God and about yourself. He will have told you what the truth is. Think of yourself as you now know Father God sees you and how He wants you to see yourself. Remember to declare your truths over yourself and then reflect on them. Journal how Father God sees you. Then go out believing these truths.*

But when the Father sends the Spirit of Holiness, the One like me who sets you free, he will teach you all the things in my name. And he will inspire you to remember every word that I've told you.
John 14:26 TPT

Date

Accepting Holy Spirit

Not everyone actually sees a picture of Holy Spirit in their Sozos. They usually have an impression of Him being present, a feeling that He's close. Was it the same for you?

We also find in Sozo that those people who have either a bad relationship or no relationship with their mothers often have a bad or no relationship with Holy Spirit. Now, why should that be? We think it's because Holy Spirit's role and the role our mothers are meant to fulfil are very similar. Mothers are meant to comfort us and make us feel secure and wrapped in love. They're also the ones from whom we get our basic learning about good and bad, safe and unsafe, and how to tie shoelaces, or cross the road safely. Holy Spirit was sent to fill those who accept Jesus as the gateway to the Father. He was sent to comfort us, to act as a moral compass, to guide us as to what's right and wrong. In John 14:25-26 ESV Jesus reassured his disciples, telling them about "The Helper, the Holy Spirit, whom the Father will send in My name, He will teach you all things, and bring to your remembrance all things that I said to you."

In other words, Holy Spirit carries all that Jesus intends for us.

In the same way that many people put their dad's face onto that of Father God, many put their mother's face onto Holy Spirit, thinking that Holy Spirit will treat them in exactly the same way. Without knowing that we're doing it, we try and protect ourselves by limiting our expectations of anything good from God to our own life experience of those who should have loved on us as God wants to. We reflect our parents'/guardians'/figures of authority's brokenness and lack of healing onto God, expecting no more from Him than we've experienced in the past. And that's not the truth! That's not who He is. As we learn to recognize and accept that His truth is very different from our experience, healing comes.

Reading:

> *But when the Father sends the Spirit of Holiness, the One like me who sets you free, he will teach you all things in my name. And he will inspire you to remember every word that I've told you.*
> JOHN 14:26 TPT

Also Read:

Romans 5:5

Prayer and Response:

> *Is there still anything you feel you need to forgive your mother for? Perhaps "need" is the wrong word. Try asking Holy Spirit if there are still any resentments or judgments left. The aim is to be completely free of anything that doesn't look like Jesus, so this is worth spending time on!*

Thank Holy Spirit for the truth that He's your comforter and teacher, that you can rely on Him, and that He's there to help.

But Christ proved God's passionate love for us by dying in our place when we were still lost and ungodly.

Romans 5:8 TPT

Date

It's All About Jesus!

How often have you heard the phrase, "It's all about Jesus?" It can be a bit of a mantra, but it's largely true. We say "largely" because Jesus' role on Earth was to act as a signpost towards Father God and to demonstrate to us all Father God's nature. So, it's all about Father God too… and Holy Spirit! But here's the deal – it was Jesus who walked amongst us, made friends, laughed, cried, and was completely human. He retains that ability to be a friend and walk alongside us. He can still laugh and weep with us. He can still be a brother to us. He can still lead us to His Father, who is Our Father. We only have to ask.

If, after your Sozo, you still feel that you need to work on your relationship with Father God or Holy Spirit, then turn to Jesus. Ask Him to join you wherever it is you're praying; He'll be there. It's for you to take a leap into an acceptance of the supernatural and to tune into His presence.

Reading:

> *But Christ proved God's passionate love for us by dying in our place when we were still lost and ungodly.*
> Romans 5:8 TPT

Also Read:

John 3:16

Psalm 116:2

Prayer and Response:

> *Ask Jesus where He is in the room you're in and then physically lean in that direction. Ask Him what He thinks of you. Tell Him what you're thinking, what's troubling you, and listen to what He thinks about it. Be ready to write down what He tells you! Thank Him for being your companion and friend. Make the decision to involve Him in your everyday life. He's there! He really is!*

Why not watch the film The Shack this week? It helps us to see God out of our box! As you watch, ask Jesus what truths He'd like you to learn about Him and about trust.

And you did not receive the "spirit of religious duty," leading you back into the fear of never being good enough. But you have received the "spirit of full acceptance," enfolding you into the family of God. And you will never feel orphaned, for as he rises up within us, our spirits join him in saying the words of tender affection, "Beloved Father!" For the Holy Spirit makes God's fatherhood real to us as he whispers into our innermost being, "You are God's beloved child!"

Romans 8:15-16 TPT

Date

Who are You? Whose are You?

Aren't those great questions? It's such an innocent looking sentence but discovering the answer and being sure of it can be most challenging! At its root, it's a question of identity and belonging, but let's start with identity. The "Who are you?" question is loaded with possibilities. Are you what you do for a living or as a past-time? Are you what your family, your friends, or even those who don't like you see you as? Has whatever you are been decided by you or by others? So often we end up being what we've been pigeon-holed as. We just let ourselves become what we're perceived to be by those who influence and possibly control us most.

That's not how it's meant to be. God didn't make us powerful and free for us to give it all away or have it stolen from us. He made us powerful and free so that we could choose Him and be powerful within the relationship of covering and love that He gives us. You will have various roles with each person in your life – a mum or dad, sister or brother, co-worker, pastor, or local street sweeper. But above these is the most important identity tag of all – you're a daughter or son of Father God, brother or sister to Jesus, sharing His DNA, and carrying it wherever you go. That's who you are!

So...Whose are you? Who do you follow? Who heads your family? Who do you look to for support and protection? Where do you turn when things are rough? Who do you feel comfortable with? Who do you belong and feel loyal to? Is it with Abba, Father God? Choose Him because He wants to protect and provide for you! He wants to be your Father.

Reading:

And you did not receive the "spirit of religious duty," leading you back into the fear of never being good enough. But you have received the "spirit of full acceptance," enfolding you into the family of God. And you will never feel orphaned, for as he rises up within us, our spirits join him in saying the words of tender affection, "Beloved Father!" For the Holy Spirit makes God's fatherhood real to us as he whispers into our innermost being, "You are God's beloved child!"
ROMANS 8:15-16 TPT

Also Read:

Galatians 3:26

Prayer and Response:

Read through the above again. Have you ever felt fully and unconditionally loved? Have you ever felt that you belong unquestionably? The truth is you are, and you do! Spend some time today asking Father God to show you what this truly looks like, allowing yourself to feel the fullness of the depth of it. You may want to ask Jesus to show you how He feels about you too – after all, you're family! Take your time. Try and write down your emotions. Let them flow. Don't be rushed.

Are you weary, carrying a heavy burden? Then come to me. I will refresh your life, for I am your oasis. Simply join your life with mine. Learn my ways and you'll discover that I'm gentle, humble, easy to please. You will find refreshment and rest in me.

Matthew 11:28–29 TPT

Date

Carrying Emotional Baggage

We all do it. We spend our early lives picking it up, and the rest of our lives either living with it or trying to get rid of it. It's the emotional baggage we all carry as a result of the wounds that life so easily inflicts on us from the moment of our conception.

Did you know that all of us carry the weight of nearly 15lb of air around with us all the time[†]? It's the weight of the earth's atmosphere pressing down on us. We're born with it and die with it. We just don't notice it, and if we're not careful, our emotional baggage will be the same. But it doesn't have to be that way! We're made in Father God's image. He's made us to be like Him. He wants us to be free of emotional baggage just as His son Jesus was. After all, we're His sons and daughters too!

Hopefully, your Sozo will have dealt with a lot of emotional baggage, and you'll have forgiven those who have wounded you, and recognized the lies you've believed about yourself because of it. It's an onion skin process – often peeling just one layer at a time. It can be painful as you recognize how believing lies about yourself has changed the way you've done life, but what freedom there is as each layer is removed! Ridding yourself of lies is a process that involves the recognition of each lie. One has to forgive the person, persons, or even organization(s) responsible, renounce the lie(s), and then ask Father God for the truth as He sees it. Declare that truth and make it your own!

[†]http://www.physics.org/facts/air-really.asp

Reading:

> *Are you weary, carrying a heavy burden? Then come to me. I will refresh your life, for I am your oasis. Simply join your life with mine. Learn my ways and you'll discover that I'm gentle, humble, easy to please. You will find refreshment and rest in me.*
> MATTHEW 11:28–29 TPT

Also Read:

Hebrews 12:1

Prayer and Response:

> *People often ask if one can Sozo oneself. The answer is "yes," to a degree. Ask Father God what lies you're believing about yourself, and He will answer you. Then ask Him what the truth is. Write this down and reflect on these truths. Declare them over yourself. Does that feel real? Sometimes our emotions have to catch up with the truth! Ultimately, our whole life should be a constant conversation with Jesus, an ongoing series of questions He answers, all cumulatively leading to our being able to be completely confident in our identity in Him.*

Sometimes, the wounds and lies are so ingrained, so part of who we are, and so familiar to us that we just can't see them. That's when it takes someone else to help us. Most Sozo practitioners have a Sozo every year! We're all determined to get rid of our baggage! Don't feel bad about having as many Sozos as it takes. It shows you're determined to deal with your stuff!

This super abundant grace is already powerfully working in us,
releasing within us all forms of wisdom and practical understanding.
Ephesians 1:8 TPT

Date

The Wonder of Grace

Recently, I saw an almost throw-away on Facebook. It said, "Favor is grace in action." The implication is that we, all of us, live with the constant promise of God's grace but that we have to somehow engage with that grace to move to the point of actually receiving it and living in favor. It's a comment that demands an understanding of grace and how it can work.

Grace is God's unconditional and unearned love and acceptance. Being grace-filled is how we should be. We shouldn't need to know and feel more than this. It's "being" not "doing."

The trouble is that many people, inside and outside the Church family, don't really understand the concept of "being." For the world outside, it's what you do that matters, not who you are. The world looks at what we achieve and measures us by that. By that yardstick, success is based on how well we've done and the level of our achievement, and that's where it can go wrong for us. Our problems start when we allow other people's recognition of our achievements to give us a sense of significance instead of knowing who we are as God's children and allowing that to give us our identity. What happens is that we begin to feel good about ourselves because of other people's opinions. Other people's admiration feeds our ego, pride, sense of self-worth, and identity. If we allow this, then our sense of significance is based on our achievements, and this becomes what sustains us and allows us to feel good about ourselves, giving the warm feeling of being accepted. Can you see how this acceptance, based on our "doing," becomes a constant treadmill of having to achieve to be accepted?

Does that make sense? Can you see how easy it is to fall for that way of looking for acceptance from the "world" rather than from God? And if you identify with this, how does this ungodly measure of acceptance make you feel?

So, if that's everyday life, how would our lives look and feel if we knew for certain in our hearts who we are and Whose we are? What would living with a covering of grace really be like?

Answer: Completely different! It's the opposite of what you've just been reading about!

As God's children, our starting point is to know and feel that we're accepted. Remember what you learned on Day 9. You've been chosen by God! You're part of His family! You're carrying His DNA! That knowledge should give us confidence. We should feel good about ourselves because we can receive a daily inflow of God's grace, His unconditional love, and Jesus' attention. Being sustained like this and being full of Him stirs up the desire in us to give back, to repay, to achieve, not for us – but for Him and for His glory! Now, how does that feel? That's grace. As you step into a life of grace, of showing others His grace in you, you'll find you're walking in His favor, grace in action, and the need to strive for acceptance from anyone other than Father God just quietly disappears.

Reading:

> *This super abundant grace is already powerfully working in us, releasing within us all forms of wisdom and practical understanding.*
> EPHESIANS 1:8 TPT

Also Read:

Hebrews 4:16

Prayer and Response:

Think and pray about what Brennan Manning wrote:

> *"Do you believe that the God of Jesus loves you beyond worthiness and unworthiness, beyond fidelity and infidelity—that He loves you in the morning sun and in the evening rain—that He loves you when your intellect denies it, your emotions refuse it, and your whole being rejects it? Do you believe that God loves without condition or reservation and loves you this moment as you are and not as you should be…?" He does, you know! He really does!*
> ALL IS GRACE: A RAGAMUFFIN MEMOIR

How do you respond to knowing you're drenched in God's love?

Can you describe the feeling well enough to be able to write it down?

And whenever you stand praying, if you find you carry something in your heart against another person, release him and forgive him so that your Father in heaven will also release you and forgive you of your faults.
Mark 11:25 TPT

Date

Forgiveness

It's said that the first to apologize is the bravest, the first to forgive is the strongest, and the first to forget is the happiest. Forgiveness isn't one of the Ten Commandments. In fact, it's not even something that's talked about very much in sermons. However, it's one of the most important factors in living healthy and free. Remember, we don't forgive to release others and make them feel better, although this happens. We choose to forgive not just because God asks us to and it's the right thing to do, we forgive because He knows that in forgiving others, we release ourselves from bitterness, anger, resentment, and retaliation.

Unforgiveness is a part of the emotional baggage we talked about on Day 10. It weighs us down, and it produces bitterness and resentment towards those who have hurt us and the world at large. It makes us angry and, at its extreme, can cause us to take unimaginable actions. Here's the rub. Those people we're holding in unforgiveness often haven't a clue either that they've hurt us to the degree they have or that we hold such enmity. They might well be amazed.

Forgiveness starts at home. It starts with you. We're often our own worst critics, and if we've ever allowed ourselves to take on responsibilities (often false ones), we can so easily beat ourselves up for not having done enough, for letting others down, or for just failing. We do all of this without it necessarily being in anyone else's opinion other than our own. When we do this, we conjure up false identities around what we think people think about us, keeping us from the relationships and intimacy that we, as humans, most desire. The healing process begins when we ask God the question, "Do I feel this way about me?"

Reading:

> *And whenever you stand praying, if you find you carry something in your heart against another person, release him and forgive him so that your Father in heaven will also release you and forgive you of your faults.*
> MARK 11:25 TPT

Also Read:

Colossians 3:13

Matthew 6:13-14

Prayer and Response:

> *How did it feel to forgive people during your Sozo? How do you feel about them now? Do you feel freer? Is there anyone else you could forgive? Ask Father God!*

Choose to forgive those He brings to your attention. Forgive them not just for what they did but how that made you feel. There could be a list, so take your time and be clear about what it is you're forgiving them for. One way to know if you've really forgiven someone is to ask yourself whether you can not only forgive that person but also bless them. Why not write your list down and go through it one by one? You could revisit this list in a month or two and see how you feel about those people then. Hopefully, you will feel very differently about them, but if not, there's more forgiveness to be done!

I – yes, I alone – will blot out your sins for my own sake and will never think of them again.
Isaiah 43:25 NLT

Date

Shame

Shame isolates us! It's a hidden secret. It doesn't like coming into the light. It makes us believe that we're constantly uncovered, and that the people surrounding us can see all the way into us. It steals our confidence and compromises our self-worth. It is the ultimate thief and liar that stops us from being authentic. We can take it on ourselves by doing what we later consider shameful, or we can carry shame as a result of what was done to us. Quite possibly one of our ancestors could be the origin of shame. Remembering that shame, as with anger, divorce, or so many repetitive patterns, can be passed down the generations as learned behavior. Either way, that shame will hold us back from being who Father God wants us to be, a beloved son or daughter, made in His image and living a life knowing who we are and Whose we are, strong in ourselves, known to God, and loved by Him.

Shame doesn't have to be as a result of something sexual. It can arise from any activity or thought that we're ashamed of, whether done by us or against us, but more often shame comes as a result of having been abused or allowing sexual sin into our lives. Abuse or sexual sin leaves one scarred. We feel dirty, worthless and unlovable, sometimes almost as if we deserved it because possibly, we believe we attracted or deserved the abuse. This is a lie! Don't take on the responsibility for another person's misbehavior.

If you have acted in a shameful way, what then? Do you feel that your action has placed you beyond God's grace? Do you feel that He's turned His back on you? The answer is up to you. If a child of yours acted awfully but was truly repentant, how would you respond? Hopefully with an acceptance based on deep love. So how much more likely is it that Father God is ready to accept a truly repentant child of His? Nothing, with true and full repentance, is beyond redemption. Whatever you might feel, the truth is that God has forgiven you. If you've been abused and have just read this paragraph, remember that we need to forgive much, because we, in turn, have been forgiven much. It may not be easy, but it's a choice that leads to release and freedom.

Reading:

> *I – yes, I alone – will blot out your sins for my own sake and will never think of them again.*
> Isaiah 43:25 NLT

Also Read:

Romans 8:1

1 John 1:9

Prayer and Response:

> *Thank Father God that He sees you and knows you better than you do and loves you none the less! Tell Him that you're determined not to partner with shame any longer. If you've dealt with shame in your Sozo, declare these truths again!*

Ask Jesus to show you what your life would look like if you were able to live it entirely free of shame. As He shows you, ask Him what stops you from experiencing that freedom. You may want to write down what He tells you so you can start to deal with whatever He's highlighted to you.

Since we are now joined to Christ, we have been given the treasures of redemption by his blood – the total cancellation of our sins – all because of the cascading riches of his grace.
EPHESIANS 1:7 TPT

Date

What's the Cost of Sin?

We talked yesterday about shame and what it can do to us. But what about sin? If shame can isolate us, the knowledge of our own sin can destroy us if we allow it. Of course, if we are addicted to that sin, then we can be completely enthralled by it while it's destroying us. That's the power of the enemy working deep within. It's insidious, thoroughly nasty, and an evil mistress.

Bethel's senior pastor, Bill Johnson, has said, "A Christian only sins because he or she believes a lie." Whatever the sin is, big or small (to you), your being caught up in it will be as a result of a lie you're believing about you, your circumstances, or your abilities. The good news is that you're no more stuck with it than the prodigal son who treated his father appallingly. He returned home truly repentant and was totally forgiven, his sin forgotten.

Jesus taught us to pray a simple little prayer, the one we call the Lord's Prayer. In it, there's the line "Forgive us our trespasses (sins)." Jesus knows full well that we will fall short but tells us that so long as we acknowledge and repent of our mistakes, we can leave sin behind us and move on. We'll be thinking more about forgiveness on Day 17.

Repenting isn't being sorry for being caught. It's a heart change that says, "I did it, and I choose to do a complete U-turn away from that sin" and puts us back where we were before we ever got caught up in it. Remember what Paul said in Romans 3:23 NIV, "For all have sinned and fall short of the glory of God." No one is alone in their sin.

Reading:

> *Since we are now joined to Christ, we have been given the treasures of redemption by his blood – the total cancellation of our sins – all because of the cascading riches of his grace.*
> Ephesians 1:7 TPT

Also Read:

Acts 3:19

Romans 8:1

Prayer and Response:

> *Determine to see yourself as a saint and not a sinner. Read the Romans 8:1 passage mentioned above and thank God for it! Thank Him that we can go to Him as a loving, compassionate Father and that He's not a finger-wagging kind of God that makes us earn our way back into His favor. Thank Him for already favoring us because of what Jesus has done. Try writing your thanks to Him as a letter.*

Stop imitating the ideals and opinions of the culture around you, but be inwardly transformed by the Holy Spirit through a total reformation of how you think. This will empower you to discern God's will as you live a beautiful life, satisfying and perfect in his eyes.

ROMANS 12:2 TPT

Date

Habits and Mindsets

Have you ever stopped to work out how much of what you do every day is habit? There's isn't anything necessarily wrong with this, but you'll find it to be a very large part of your daily routine. It's not just how you fill your time; it's the way you do life – the same cup, the same coffee, the same amount of milk or no milk, the same way of stirring, and with the same hand. Then there's the origin of the habit. Where did it come from? When did it start? Where did you learn it? It's an interesting thought that we are quite possibly replicating some of the habits that our forefathers had, passed down the generations.

So what? Well, our thinking can be habitual too, and that's what we're looking at today. How much of your thinking is due to ungodly mindsets and habitual ways of thinking about things that negatively determine your reaction to life? It's what Bill Johnson calls "stinking thinking."

How does this apply to Sozo?

We know that we learn most of our thought patterns and self-beliefs in our early formative years, largely from our parents and siblings, and that these settle and become part of who we are. Our Sozo sessions help us to recognize and identify the wounds we've unconsciously taken on and the consequent lies we've believed about ourselves because of this"stinking thinking". It's not our just parents and siblings. It can be as a result of having no parents or the wrong sort of authority figures. A throw-away playground catcall can be enough to allow a negative thought pattern to take root by allowing a wrong self-belief to become a part of who we are. And...they're all lies that have wounded us, with each lie taking us one step further away from our destiny and true identity in Christ.

In your Sozo, as each lie was revealed and replaced with God's truth, the right for those lies to remain with you was removed. That's the deliverance element of Sozo as it works to deliver us from the lies the enemy uses to try and control us, and from the demonic influences attached to these lies.

The snag is believing and receiving it! It's up to each of us whether we leave our Sozo session in the same state and believing the same lies as when we arrived, or whether we leave believing all the truths we heard. It's entirely our choice. It's also our choice how we now handle the habits and mindsets we had before our Sozo. The right for those lies to influence us was removed during our Sozo. However, we still have to deal with any habits and mindsets characterized by those lies. If we don't get rid of these, we'll be giving life back to the lies and allowing them to become part of us again. That's why making declarations about the truth of who we are in Father God's eyes is so important.

Reading:

> *Stop imitating the ideals and opinions of the culture around you, but be inwardly transformed by the Holy Spirit through a total reformation of how you think. This will empower you to discern God's will as you live a beautiful life, satisfying and perfect in his eyes.*
> Romans 12:2 TPT

Also Read:

Ephesians 4:24

Prayer and Response:

> *Some habits and mindsets will have formed as a result of the lies that you used to believe about yourself. Identify these and make the choice not to partner any longer with the way those lies have surfaced as unhelpful behavior in your daily life. Start with a couple that have had a significant effect. When you recognize them re-occurring, ask Jesus how He would have you behave or react in that situation. Then do it! You'll find that as you start to deal with the "big" lies and habits, the lesser ones will just fade away. You may also find that writing these down and seeing them in front of you will help you clarify your response. You could also renounce those lies by asking Jesus what the opposite is or how He sees things. Then use what you hear as a declaration.*

The Spirit of the Sovereign Lord is on me, because the Lord has anointed me to proclaim good news to the poor. He has sent me to bind up the broken-hearted, to proclaim freedom for the captives and release from darkness for the prisoners.
Isaiah 61:1 NIV

Date

"Captive" or Prisoner? Part One

In Luke 4:18, Jesus is quoting Isaiah when He tells us that:

> *The Spirit of the Sovereign Lord is on me, because the Lord has anointed me to proclaim good news to the poor. He has sent me to bind up the broken-hearted (those with shattered minds), to proclaim freedom (liberty) for the captives and release from darkness (freedom) for the prisoners.*
> ISAIAH 61:1 NIV PARENTHESIS MINE.

It's clear that Jesus is differentiating between "captives" and "prisoners." The essence of being a captive is that we've been captured. We, ourselves, don't necessarily have to do anything wrong to be in this position. We could just have been in the wrong place or the right place at the wrong time. It's not hard to imagine a child being tainted or cursed by the negative spiritual atmosphere they're growing up in and by what's going on around them. The truth is that simply by living in a fallen world we can be affected negatively either as a result of people's sin to us or by circumstances. We can fall captive by reading or watching ungodly content. It doesn't have to be sexual. It's whatever has a hold on us and acts as a barrier to us believing and accepting the fullness of God's outrageous love. We can become a captive by sin in our generational line that's been handed down as a way of seeing or doing life. It's not difficult.

Here's the good news. If today, you still feel that you are a captive, it's also not difficult to set yourself free. It can be as easy as brushing dog hairs off a jacket. The enemy's hold can be broken off with a short prayer such as "I break off the spirit of (whatever it is that's been identified, anger for instance) and impart peace." Remember to pray in the opposite to replace whatever it is that you're breaking the power of.

Reading:

> *Now my beloved ones, I have saved these most complicated truths for last: Be supernaturally infused with strength through your life-union with the Lord Jesus. Stand victorious with the force of his explosive power flowing in and through you.*
> *Put on God's complete set of armor provided for us, so that you will be protected as you fight against the evil strategies of the accuser!*
> *Your hand-to-hand combat is not with human beings, but with the highest principalities and authorities operating in rebellion under the heavenly realms. For they are a powerful class of demon-gods and evil spirits that hold the dark world in bondage. Because of this you must wear all the armor that God provides so that you're protected as you confront the slanderer, for you are destined for all things and will rise victorious.*
> *Put on truth to strengthen you to stand in triumph. Put on holiness as the protective armor that covers your heart. Stand on your feet alert, then you'll always be ready to share the blessings of peace.*
> *In every battle, take faith as your wrap-around shield, for it is able to extinguish the blazing arrows coming at you from the Evil One!*
> *Embrace the power of salvation's full deliverance, like a helmet to protect your thoughts from lies. And take the mighty razor-sharp Spirit-sword of the spoken word of God.*
> *Pray passionately in the Spirit, as you constantly intercede with every form of prayer at all times. Pray the blessing of God on all his believers.*
> EPHESIANS 6:10–18 TPT

Prayer and Response:

We mentioned the words "spiritual atmosphere" above. This may be a phrase you're not familiar with. If we believe that we live in a supernatural world where miracles can and do happen, then a spiritual atmosphere is what each of us lives in all the time – we're just not always aware of it. Once you are, then you can change it. Take time to discern the spiritual atmosphere you spend each element of your life in. If it's ungodly, pray for the opposite to replace it. You'll be amazed at the difference a simple, heartfelt prayer can make. Dawna de Silva's teaching on Shifting Atmospheres is excellent. Make a note of the atmospheres that you feel, along with where and how they change as you pray the opposite.

So, My heavenly Father also will do to you if each of you, from his heart, does not forgive his brother his trespasses.
MATTHEW 18:35 NIV

Date

"Captive or "Prisoner?" Part Two

If, after praying yesterday, you don't feel a release, it's possible that you're a prisoner and not a captive. This might have happened by you partnering with sin or maybe by not forgiving those who have sinned against you. One way or another, it will be a choice you've made or a sin you've committed rather than what has been done to you. This being the case, your prison, be it of unforgiveness or self-inflicted sin, is of your own making. It's harder to become free because you have to do the work by making another choice – this time to break the link with sin or to forgive, however hard it may be.

You'll probably know the parable of the unforgiving servant in Matthew 18:21-35. The essence of it is that the servant wanted mercy for himself but justice for others. However, the truth is that you can't have it both ways. This is made clear as the story goes on from verse 32 NIV:

> 32*Then his master, after he had called him, said to him, 'You wicked servant! I forgave you all that debt because you begged me.* 33*Should you not also have had compassion on your fellow servant, just as I had pity on you?'* 34*And his master was angry, and delivered him to the torturers until he should pay all that was due to him.*

And here's the attention grabber for us:

> 35*So, My heavenly Father also will do to you if each of you, from his heart, does not forgive his brother his trespasses.*

Surely, it's the person who has done the wrong that should go to prison! You would think so, but with unforgiveness, that's not what happens. What unforgiveness does is put us in our own silent prison! What happens is that in our lonely cell we get sick, bitterness overwhelms us, loneliness pervades, strained relationships occur, and irrational fears multiply. We become hostages to sin, suffer outbursts of anger, and inevitably, distance ourselves from God.

What's sad is that some of us wrongly think that our suffering is somehow hurting those who have hurt us, but it isn't. It is only hurting us. We think we're punishing them, but they're not in prison – we are! We think forgiveness is an act of kindness to others and of course, it is, but it's also an act of kindness to ourselves! When we remove the hook of unforgiveness from our hearts, we free ourselves because we are no longer bound to that person. By not forgiving, we remain hooked to the pain of the past. To be able to truly forgive, it helps to dwell on the extent to which we, ourselves, have been forgiven and how Jesus loves us through our sin. If we can accept His grace for ourselves, it empowers us to release judgments we hold over those who have sinned against us. As we receive His grace, it becomes easier to release our grace.

All of which is to say, forgiveness is a command. It's not a feeling. It's not optional. It's meant to be a lifestyle for all Christians. It's essential. If this is resonating with you, maybe it's time to truly forgive those who have wounded you...

Reading:

> *Later Peter approached Jesus and said, "How many times do I have to forgive my fellow believer who keeps offending me? Seven times?" Jesus answered, "Not seven times, Peter, but seventy times seven times!"*
>
> MATTHEW 18:21-22 TPT

Also Read:

Ephesians 4:31-32

Prayer and Response:

> *Forgiveness is a process. Sometimes, we think and feel that we've forgiven everyone there is to forgive and for everything they ever did to us. Then some memory returns, hits us, and reminds us of another offense against us. As you were reading through this, was Holy Spirit*

highlighting any areas of unforgiveness in your heart that you should deal with now? It's your choice whether you do so. You can do it! Make a note of those you're prompted to forgive. As names are revealed to you, ask Holy Spirit specifically what you need to forgive that person for and how it made you feel. You may be surprised how Holy Spirit takes you to the root of an issue and how you were made to feel by what happened is more important than the action itself.

Keep journaling! When you come to read your journal again in the future, you'll be amazed at how your attitude and thinking will have changed.

Lift up a great shout of joy to the Lord!
Go ahead and do it – everyone, everywhere!
Psalm 100: 1 TPT

Date

Here We Are to Worship

There's a common misunderstanding that worship means the same as singing songs or hymns. It doesn't!

At its most basic, worship is simply the act of adoring God. It is expressing our love of Him to Him from the heart. How you do that is very much up to you. Most of us find it quite hard to concentrate our minds long enough on adoring God to make it feel that we've done it significantly. Additionally, for many of us, our ability to actually express love in any meaningful way is really limited, especially if our experience of receiving love from anyone is equally limited. Sometimes, we can hardly find a way to tell our nearest and dearest that we love them, let alone God.

How can we get over this? One way is through worship music. People talk about using worship music to soak, allowing the music to wash over and fill you as you spend time relaxing with God, and that's fine. However, the act of worship is much more intentional and, using songs as a means to do this, gives us the opportunity to engage completely with the words and allows us to express our hearts in singing. Furthermore, it just doesn't matter how bad your voice is because what God hears is the intent, the meaning, and the heart-thought behind the noise. That's why King David's scampering around pleased the Lord. He worshipped with complete abandon, giving himself entirely to adoration.

There's so much more though. If you can train yourself to recognize beauty in life and creation and thank the God who created that moment, that view, that experience, that in itself is worship. Recognizing God's hand in both the smallest detail and the obvious pleasure is acknowledgement of Him in our lives and, in itself, worship. Imagine if you could carry an awareness of God's love for you in each breath, that would be worship.

Reading:

Lift up a great shout of joy to the Lord!
Go ahead and do it – everyone, everywhere!
As you serve him, be glad and worship him.
Sing your way into his presence with joy!
And realize what this really means-
we have the privilege of worshipping the Lord our God.
For he is our Creator and we belong to him.
We are the people of his pleasure.
You can pass through his open gates with the password of praise.
Come right into his presence with thanksgiving.
Come bring your thank offering to him
And affectionately bless his beautiful name!
For the Lord is always good and ready to receive you.
He's so loving that it will amaze you-
So kind that it will astound you!
And he is famous for his faithfulness towards all.
PSALM 100 [TPT]

Also Read:

John 4:23-24

Prayer and Response:

Speaking in tongues is also worship! Speaking out a Psalm of praise is as well. Try praying Psalm 145 to Father God as if He was standing in front of you.

Not everyone speaks in tongues. If you don't you might feel cautious, but don't be overcautious. After all, the Bible calls the ability to speak in tongues a spiritual gift. In Mark's Gospel, we read Jesus telling us "And these signs will follow those who believe … they will speak with new tongues." If it's something you'd like to do, then remember that God does not possess or force you to speak in tongues automatically. You have to initiate the process. Just start speaking sounds, keep it going, and do not stop. You have to form the words and give them the push so that it comes out. God will not do it for you, but Holy Spirit will help if you ask Him. You don't need to think about what words to speak as God is always there. Just move your mouth and speak out loud boldly. Make a note of your progress. You'll be glad you did when you come to look back.

When you judge others, and then do the same things they do, you condemn yourself.
Romans 2:2 TPT

Date

Judgments

The first verses of Romans 2 really say all there is to know about judgments:

> *No matter who you are, before you judge the wickedness of others, you had better remember this: you are also without excuse, for you too are guilty of the same kind of things! When you judge others, and then do the same things they do, you condemn yourself.*
> Romans 2:1-2 TPT

The trouble is, we do it anyway. Why? One reason is that we use judgment to protect ourselves. If we can come to a negative conclusion about someone or what they've done, then that someone has no power over us. In our minds, they've been dealt with and disempowered. Whatever they say or do can't harm us and doesn't matter because we've already pigeon-holed them to a place where they have become unimportant to us. For example, if we've judged a car, a house, a vacation, and/or a school to be no good, it doesn't matter that we can't afford it.

In doing this, we condemn ourselves. Our job as a Christian is to encourage, not to knock down. It is to love, not to belittle. However, we can only love to the degree that we, ourselves, feel loved. We can only encourage if we have the experience of being encouraged. If that hasn't happened in our childhood, then it is God who will fill in and flood us with His love and encouragement if we ask Him and let Him. It's up to us.

So, how do we not judge? We stop at observation. One can observe a situation without judging it. Similarly, one can talk about a person without passing an opinion because that opinion is a judgment! Here's the deal... even a positive judgment is best avoided because the moment you set someone up as being a great leader, mother, teacher, or cook, the only direction they can travel is to fail and let you down. Once you're aware of how easy it is to fall into judgment, you'll recognize how much of it we do. You might be surprised.

Reading:

> *1Refuse to be a critic full of bias toward others, and judgment will not be passed on you.*
> *2For you'll be judged by the same standard that you've used to judge others. The measurement you use on them will be used on you.*
> *3Why would you focus on the flaw in someone else's life and yet fail to notice the glaring flaws of your own?*
> *4How could you say to your friend, 'Let me show you where you're wrong,' when you're guilty of even more?*
> *5You're being hypercritical and a hypocrite! First acknowledge your own 'blind spots' and deal with them, and then you'll be capable of dealing with the 'blind spot' of your friend.*
> MATTHEW 7:1–5 TPT

Also Read:

Luke 6:37

Romans 2:1

Prayer and Response:

What would a life free of judgments look like? What if one was purposeful and determined to only see the gold in people and to try and bring that out? How would that change your every day? Try it! Ask Jesus to show you those people or situations you've judged and what that judgment was based on. Ask Him to show you how He sees those people or things. Make a note of who and what He shows you and determine to pray positively for them. Watch to see how your relationship with those people changes.

Listen to my testimony: I cried to God in my distress and he answered me. He freed me from all my fears!
Psalm 34:4 TPT

Date

Dealing with Fear

If there's one theme that will almost inevitably turn up in a Sozo, it's fear. It doesn't have to be called "fear." It can show up as anxiety, worry, or stress, but in whatever shape it turns up, fear casts a shadow over us. Its consequences can completely change the course of our lives. It can cause us to need to control events around us. It can lead us to harmful addictions or even self-harm and all such things are aimed at somehow masking or diverting fear and allowing us to hide from it for a while.

> *You don't need to be told that fear is not God's intention. His perfect love casts out all fear*
> 1 John 4:18

Oddly, it's often the case that the fear we carry isn't our own. In other words, we're not fearful as a justifiable result of what has happened to us; we're fearful because we've learned it from someone else, usually a parent. If your mother was a fearful lady, especially when she was carrying you, then it's more than likely that you'll have been born and have grown up in an atmosphere of fear. No wonder it's lingered. If that sounds odd, think of how much of what you do mirrors or copies some action or behavior your parents did. You probably didn't set out to copy that mannerism, but you do it anyway. The same is true, not just for what you could see to copy but also for the unseen things that were a part of them as well. If not your parents, then it was whomever most influenced you growing up.

Hopefully, your Sozo will have dealt with at least some, if not most or all, of the fears from the past that you were carrying. Today, why not just check to see whether any fear still clouds your life? Ask Father God whether you're still carrying any fear or anxiety. If the answer is "yes," then ask Him what lie you're believing and whether there's anyone who needs to be forgiven attached to that lie. Then forgive the person concerned, not just for the event, but for the feelings of fear you've carried as a consequence. Renounce that lie and ask Father God for the truth. Then journal the truth. You don't have to live with fear. If you sense that it's lingering, don't feel bad about scheduling another Sozo. Most of us who minister Sozo have our own Sozos regularly. It's like giving your car a regular service.

Reading:

> *Listen to my testimony: I cried to God in my distress and he answered me. He freed me from all my fears!*
> PSALM 34:4 TPT

Also Read:

Psalm 94:19

John 14:27

1 John 4:18

Prayer and Response:

Take the above readings and use the truths contained as a starting point for a prayer. It could be something like this:

Father God, today I declare that I did not receive the spirit of bondage to fear, but I receive the Spirit of Adoption to cry "Abba Father." Thank you, Father God, for delivering me from all my fears. Today, I release peace and comfort into my heart. You could write your prayer down and return to it regularly.

My dearest brothers and sisters, take this to heart: Be quick to listen, but slow to speak. And be slow to become angry, for human anger is never a legitimate tool to promote God's righteous purpose.
JAMES 1:19–20 TPT

Date

How Anger Works

Did you know that very often anger is a learned behavior? There aren't many people who are naturally and inherently angry, and (before you say it or even think it) there's no known reason why redheads should have a temper other than the fact that they probably learned it from their red-headed parent!

It's a great shield though. Temper protects one from being hurt; it stops other people from getting too close. It can put you in control and allow you to impose your will. Anger seems powerful.

Then there's righteous anger. Jesus had this when he threw the money lenders out of the Temple. Any time you've felt disturbed and angry at life's injustices, that's righteous anger. If it causes you to do something (legal) about whatever it is, that is well and good, but that's not the anger we're concerned with here.

Ask yourself the following questions: Have you allowed anger to become a friend? Do you allow it to pop up when you feel yourself being threatened? How about when someone doesn't agree with you, or when you feel they're getting the better of you? Do you use it to hurt people or to get revenge? Do you make sure that whatever you want to get done gets done your way? If so, it's time for it to go!

Reading:

> *My dearest brothers and sisters, take this to heart: Be quick to listen, but slow to speak. And be slow to become angry, for human anger is never a legitimate tool to promote God's righteous purpose.*
> JAMES 1:19–20 TPT

Also Read:

Ephesians 4:26 – 27

Proverbs 15:1

Prayer and Response:

> *If the answer to any of the questions in today's study was "yes," then what does Father God say about it? Does He feel you need anger to protect yourself? What would your life look like without anger? Could you still be safe? If anger has remained after your Sozo, then why not talk to Father God about it. Ask Him what lie(s) you are still believing about anger. You might be amazed at what He tells you. Then ask Him what the truth is and write it down!*

"For I know the plans I have for you," says the Lord. "They are plans for good and not for disaster, to give you a future and a hope. In those days when you pray I will listen. If you look for me wholeheartedly you will find me. I will be found by you," says the Lord.

Jeremiah 29:11-14a NLT

Date

Where is Hope?

Can there be hope without faith, or can there be faith without hope?

For a moment, imagine yourself as a bottle, full of all that you are, your thoughts, hopes, loves, fears, your experiences, and your memories. How much of the bottle would be full of hope, light, and Jesus, and how much of it would still be filled with the murky residue of the baggage we spoke about on Day 10?

Romans 5:2–7 has quite a lot to say about hope. It tells us that hope is the product of character, and in turn, that character comes from perseverance and perseverance from suffering. St. Paul tells us this just after saying that he/we boast in the hope of the glory of God. So where does all that leave us? Is it saying that the only way to have hope in our lives is to start by suffering? No, it isn't. But what it is saying is that if your life has included suffering and if it's left you carrying baggage, then by persevering with that baggage, by not turning your back on it but being determined to deal with it, you develop/acquire the strength of character that enables you to see hope, light, and Jesus-in spite of everything.

Paul Manwaring, one of Bethel's senior leaders, has said that there cannot be revival without inner healing. Why? It is because our ability to give to others, to shine out God's light, to carry it, and be hopeful is determined by the amount of light within us. Therefore, we can only give out to the degree that we, ourselves, are healed up and carry faith and hope, both of which are refined through perseverance.

Reading:

> *"For I know the plans I have for you," says the Lord. "They are plans for good and not for disaster, to give you a future and a hope. In those days when you pray I will listen. If you look for me wholeheartedly you will find me. I will be found by you," says the Lord.*
>
> Jeremiah 29:11-14a NLT

Also Read:

Psalm 3:4-6

Isaiah: 40:31

Prayer and Response:

Read through today's verses again. This time declare them over yourself as truths. Here is an example:

Thank you, Father God, that my hope is in You.

Thank you, God that You have good plans for me, to prosper and not to harm me. Thank You that Your plans are to give me a hope and a future. Today I choose to call out to You and to pray to You because I know You will listen to me. As I seek You with all my heart, I will be found by You, Father God.

Write down how declaring these truths makes you feel.

...for God will judge sexual immorality in any form, whether single or married.

Hebrews 13:4b TPT

Date

Avoiding Sexual Sin

Sex is an issue which almost inevitably crops up in a Sozo session! Additionally, sex can be an area of some confusion because a person may or may not necessarily be aware of which acts and thoughts constitute sexual sin and which are innocent. For example, there's a difference between being actively engaged in sexual sin and worrying that you might be tempted. After all, is temptation, or an awareness of temptation, a sexual sin? Then there's what we were talking about a few days ago – the difference between being a Captive and Prisoner. To top it all, there's shame – another topic we looked at some days ago.

Starting with shame, let's try and unpack this in as much as these things relate to sexual sin. Shame can hold us as both Captive and Prisoner depending on whether something was done to us or by us. Especially when it comes to sexual issues, shame is like an evil honey; it will stick to us and try to hold us in its grip. If you're reading this and not actively engaged in sexual sin but still feeling shame, then go back to Day 13 and read through it again paying special attention to your own notes. Here's the point – however bad things might have been, God does not want you to live your life in shame. What parent would want that for their child?

If you were a prisoner of sexual sin and it came up in your Sozo, don't feel condemned if you were caught up in it one way or another. You have been forgiven and redeemed. David called out to God, "Wash me and I will be whiter than snow." (Psalm 51:7 NIV) and he was. And so are you!

Let's get back to the question of whether an awareness of temptation is actually a sexual sin. Someone once said, "Opportunity knocks, but temptation leans on the doorbell," and that's the truth of it. Most of us know our limitations but are easily led to either push them or in weakness, ignore them. It is far better never to allow yourself to be in the position where opportunity can even knock.

Reading:

> *…for God will judge sexual immorality in any form, whether single or married.*
> HEBREWS 13:4B TPT

Also Read:

Psalm 51

1 Corinthians 6:13

Prayer and Response:

Do you remember reading about breaking habits and mindsets on Day 15? Closing the door to sexual sin can be one of the hardest of these to break, especially when life is full of temptation. God made man and woman to be beautiful. There's no harm in admiring beauty, but there is danger in wanting to taste and possess it. Read through Psalm 51 again and make it both a prayer and a declaration. Personalize it for yourself.

If shame is something that lingers like a black cloud that just won't shift, ask Jesus to show you how He took that shame upon Himself so that you won't have to live with it. He paid the price, so don't let His death be in vain in this area of your life. As He reveals the full extent of what He chose to do for you, that cloud will lift. It isn't yours to live under.

Whenever my busy thoughts were out of control, the soothing comfort of your presence calmed me down and overwhelmed me with delight.
PSALM 94:19 TPT

Date

Contentment, Happiness, and Joy

It was Aristotle, the Greek philosopher, who wrote, "Happiness is the meaning and purpose of life, the whole aim and end of human existence."

Would you agree with him? It would be easy to, but think about this – happiness, according to Aristotle, depends on what's going on around you. Your happiness will depend on the circumstances you're in… your work, your friends, your ability to make ends meet, to take vacations, to have a car, etc. Happiness, when you think about it, is up to others. Aristotle missed that the whole aim and end of human existence is not happiness but joy. Joy is deeper. Joy is a gift from God, a feeling of inner gladness, of deep-seated pleasure, and as with any other gift from God, it's a blessing. Joy is, as CS Lewis puts it, "The serious business of heaven." It's a fruit that grows as we spend time with Hcly Spirit.

The Amplified Bible describes joy as being: "happy, to be envied, and spiritually prosperous – with life-joy and satisfaction in God's favor and salvation, regardless of their outward conditions"

Now consider "contentment." Many of us settle for contentment. We put up with life as it is… our job, our home, maybe even our spouse, because that's the way it is, and that's the way it's likely to stay. Occasionally, maybe, a situation occurs which adds a little something to contentment, and for as long as it's there, we're happy. But experiencing joy – how does that work?

Reading:

Whenever my busy thoughts were out of control, the soothing comfort of your presence calmed me down and overwhelmed me with delight.
PSALM 94:19 TPT

Also Read:

Romans 15:13

Prayer and Response:

Do you think that God made you to be just content or content with occasional happiness? Or, do you think that God's desire for you is to live a joy-filled life with Him? Do you think that maybe He has a plan for you and that maybe the plan has a destiny attached to it? A plan with a destiny attached that will make the most of the talents that He's given you!

What would that be like? Ask Him! Ask Him whether He has a joy-filled plan and destiny for you. The truth is that's exactly what He has for you, me, and all of His children. He has a plan and a destiny that will fill your life with His joy. So, don't be content, seek out His plan, and step into your destiny.

How big a role does joy play in your life? What makes you genuinely joyful? Make a list and spend some time working out what exactly it is in these things that brings you joy. Then ask Father God to help you find even more.

So be alert to your brother's condition, and if you see him going the wrong direction, cry out and correct him. If there is true repentance on his part, forgive him. No matter how many times in one day your brother sins against you and says, "I'm sorry; I am changing; forgive me," you need to forgive him each and every time.

LUKE 17:2B–4 TPT

Date

Living Unoffended

It's said, "Offense is the number one weapon of the enemy," and it's certainly true that offense is guaranteed to get between one person and another and cause trouble. Sadly, this is as true in Christian circles as anywhere else. Think of just about any split between one group of people and another that you've heard of or been involved in and, at the root of it, you'll find a disagreement that has led to one or the other of the parties taking offense which invariably results in disagreements and hurt.

You could write a complete book on the subject of offense, but here are just two points for today:

- Offense is cumulative. If someone has acted oddly towards us or has appeared a little rude or maybe ignored us a couple of times, then by the time we see them again we're already expecting a repeat of some kind. Whatever they say or do will only compound the impression that's already brewing in us. They may be blissfully unaware of the offense they've caused us, but to us, it's become a major issue.

- Think about this. One cannot give offense; it can only be received! However objectionable someone might be to us, it's our choice whether we accept or receive the offense. The stronger we are in who and Whose we are, the less we will take offense, no matter what's thrown at us.

Reading:

So be alert to your brother's condition, and if you see him going the wrong direction, cry out and correct him. If there is true repentance on his part, forgive him. No matter how many times in one day your brother sins against you and says, "I'm sorry; I am changing; forgive me," you need to forgive him each and every time.

Luke 17:2b-4 TPT

Also Read:

Ecclesiastes 7:21

Proverbs 19:11

Prayer and Response:

Think about the persecution and lies that were directed at Jesus, the judgments made over Him, the unkindness, and the personal attacks. Then think of His response and how He dealt with it all. He had the choice to be offended and respond from a position of offense, but He never did.

Why not write a personal declaration so that in the future you will refuse to take offense! You may want to ask Jesus to help make a list of all those people who you feel have offended you. Can you forgive them? Make the choice to do so. Remember that forgiveness is a process. The first step is to decide to forgive – however much you don't feel you mean it!

We can demolish every deceptive fantasy that opposes God and break through every arrogant attitude that is raised up in defiance of the true knowledge of God. We capture, like prisoners of war, every thought and insist that it bow in obedience to the Anointed One.

2 Corinthians 10:5 TPT

Date

Dealing with Walls

What's funny about walls is that they don't always look like walls. Perhaps an explanation will help. In Sozo terms, a wall is what we either knowingly or unknowingly put between ourselves and God. It acts as a block that stops us from having a relationship with Him.

Did a wall come up in your Sozo? What effect was it having on your life? Did you even know it was there? Very often walls are familiar to us. We've lived with them for so long that we don't even know that they're there, but it's amazing how good it feels when they are demolished! Here's what's interesting…a wall can feel huge, impenetrable, even unmovable, like it will never go, and yet when you ask Father God to give you a tool to remove it, He gives you just the right thing. That wall is removed and falls away with hardly any effort. Father God doesn't want walls between you and Him. It's not He who builds them – it's us, and He can't wait to help us tear them down!

Reading:

[4]For although we live in the natural realm, we don't wage a military campaign employing human weapons, using manipulation to achieve our aims. Instead, our spiritual weapons are energized with divine power to effectively dismantle the defenses behind which people hide.

[5]We can demolish every deceptive fantasy that opposes God and break through every arrogant attitude that is raised up in defiance of the true knowledge of God. We capture, like prisoners of war, every thought and insist that it bow in obedience to the Anointed One.

[6]Since we are armed with such dynamic weaponry, we stand ready to punish any trace of rebellion, as soon as you choose complete obedience.
2 CORINTHIANS 10:4-6 TPT

Also Read:

James 5:16

Prayer and Response:

What do walls look like? You may not have one, but in your response time today, close your eyes and ask Father God if there's any sort of blockage or wall between you and Him. If you sense that there is, ask Him to show you what it looks like. It could take any form from a length of barbed wire to a dense fog or even a wall. Ask Him to show you where He is in relation to the wall, and then if He's on the other side, to give you whatever you need to take that wall away. Note that you may have to forgive someone for having caused you to have put that wall in place before it comes down and that someone may be yourself!

We are convinced that everyone fathered by God does not make sinning a way of life, because the Son of God protects the child of God, and the Evil One cannot touch him.
1 John 5:18 TPT

Date

The Power of the Occult

Let's start by making it clear that we believe in a big God and a little devil. That's not to say that we should completely discount satan and his works, but it is to say that we should never give him too much credence. The devil will take any opportunity he's given to wreak havoc and overtake our lives. It's our job to make sure that we do whatever we can to stop him.

You'll not need to be told, so forgive us for mentioning it anyway, that dabbling in any sort of black magic or taking part in fortune telling, séances, Tarot, Ouija boards, and even Yoga† is inviting trouble. No matter how innocent and "fun" these things appear or are made to look, there is so much more. Secret societies, specifically the Masonic Order and others modeled on it, lead their members to make word curses over themselves and future generations. Witchcraft has always been there but is becoming braver in letting itself be seen. Black magic exists. There will always be those who seek to have power over others, no matter where that power comes from.

What are we to do? Believe! Have faith! Reject the lies! Know the truth of who you are and Whose you are. King David says:

> *I hold myself in quiet and silence, like a little child in its mother's arms, like a little child, so I keep myself.*
> PSALM 131:2 TJB

David was a man who knew the ups and downs of life and constantly returned to the truth of his identity in God. The occult has no power over us unless we believe otherwise. If we reject the occult, it is beaten. Fear is the only currency it has, and if you allow it to make you feel fearful, it will hold you to itself. Remember that there's power in using the name of Jesus.

†Yoga is one of the six orthodox schools of Hindu philosophical tradition. In origin it is a group of physical, mental and spiritual practices. These practices are so intertwined that one invariably involves the others. (Wikipedia)

Reading:

We are convinced that everyone fathered by God does not make sinning a way of life, because the Son of God protects the child of God, and the Evil One cannot touch him.
1 John 5:18 TPT

Also Read:

2 Corinthians 10:4-5

Prayer and Response:

Do you realize just how powerful Jesus is? How does having Him within you make a difference as you live in our very secular world? How can you use His power to combat satan's schemes? Remember that you're more than a conqueror (Romans 8:37)! Spend some time thinking about any ungodly aspects in your everyday life and use the power of Jesus in you to pray against them. If you have a family, pray protection over them too. Write your prayer down as a declaration.

"And tell John that the blessing of heaven comes upon those who never lose their faith in me – no matter what happens!"
Matthew 11:6 TPT

Date

Is it Real?

It was St. Augustine who said:

Lord Jesus, don't let me lie when I say I love you, and protect me, for today I could betray you.

What did he mean? In essence, it's that we all struggle! Sozo is based on the belief that it's real, that Father God, Jesus, and Holy Spirit are real, love us and want to be in constant contact with us. The problem is that our belief can be, and often is, tested daily. Every day we can battle with loneliness, depression, feelings of failure and inadequacy, rejection, and fatigue. Every day we can experience the hurt when someone we trust lets us down, and every day we can question whether faith is real. Somehow, God accepts our doubt. Jesus didn't berate His disciples for being doubtful about Him. There was no ultimatum in which He told His disciples to believe in me or else. He wanted to help them to believe. He even encouraged "doubting" Thomas to put his hand into His pierced side just to help him believe (John 20:24-29).

If you feel doubt, don't worry; we all do at some point. Bill Johnson tells us, "Faith is not the absence of doubt. It is the presence of belief." God knows your doubt and values your openness with Him. He can use your doubt as the stepping stone to faith. You start out where you are, but God does not leave you where you are. Continue to reach out to Him in your prayers, your reading, and journaling, and He will most certainly reach out to you in return.

Reading:

> *"And tell John that the blessing of heaven comes upon those who never lose their faith in me – no matter what happens!"*
> MATTHEW 11:6 TPT

Also Read:

John 20:27

James 1:6-7

Prayer and Response:

> *What's the remedy to doubt? It's the truth, whether you feel it or not. That's why it's so important to declare the truths God has given you in your Sozo. As you do so, you're edifying and building yourself up, and as you do it, you'll find that doubt's hold on you begins to fade. Ask Jesus to give you a physical evidence of His existence within the next few days – something you can recognize as being Him, and He will.*

I would be delighted if you all spoke in tongues, but I desire even more that you impart prophetic revelation to others.
1 Corinthians 14: 5 [TPT]

Date

Paying It Forward – Now It's Your Turn!

One of the many blessings that you should be enjoying as a result of your Sozo is the ability to hear from and have relationship with Father God, Jesus, and Holy Spirit. If you're not confident about this, then stop right now and ask Father God what the lie is that you're still believing about Him. Our guess is that the first thing you'll hear is that you don't believe that you can hear Him! The truth will be that you most certainly can.

Is this wonderful gift of hearing from God just for you or should you be sharing it? If you're able to hear for yourself, can you also hear for others? The simple answer is "yes." You most certainly can! Do we suggest you go out onto the street and start telling people what you're hearing for them? No, we don't. Do we suggest that you start to practice this ability and test it out amongst friends? Yes, we do!

Does hearing for others make you a prophet? No, but it doesn't mean you're not. After all, it's a long journey from being a student driver to racing Formula One cars. Some make it all the way to being considered a prophet and having that role placed on them by those who know and trust them. Most of us get to bless others in our everyday lives when we consciously take the time to ask God what He wants to say to the person in front of us and then faithfully tell them what we've heard. If you're new to this here's some advice, always start by saying, "I think I'm hearing…" or "I think what God is saying..." Never "God says…!"

If all this is taking you out of your comfort zone, there are two truths you might want to bear in mind. One is that the Apostle Paul made it clear that he expected everyone to be able to prophesy, (1 Corinthians 14:31) and that prophecy is important in the Church. The second is that all of us need to be constantly stretching our faith, and that if we don't stretch our faith, we're not taking enough risks.

Reading:

It is good that you are enthusiastic and passionate about spiritual gifts, especially prophecy. When someone speaks in tongues, no one understands a word he says, because he's not speaking to people, but to God – he is speaking intimate mysteries in the Spirit. But when someone prophesies, he speaks to encourage people, to build them up, and to bring them comfort. The one who speaks in tongues advances his own spiritual progress, while the one who prophesies builds up the church. I would be delighted if you all spoke in tongues, but I desire even more that you impart prophetic revelation to others. Greater gain comes through the one who prophesies than the one who speaks in tongues, unless there is interpretation so that it builds up the entire church.

1 Corinthians 14:1-5 TPT

Prayer and Response:

As you go about your routine today, keep asking God what He wants to say to any of the people you meet. You may sense or see or feel something or an item of their clothing or jewelry may speak to you. Ask God for an interpretation so you can be specific in what you say to them. Then, go for it! Many Churches hold prophetic training events. Try one! You'll enjoy it!

Give generously and generous gifts will be given back to you, shaken down to make more room for more. Abundant gifts will pour out upon you with such an overflowing measure that it will run over the top! Your measurement of generosity becomes the measurement of your return.

Luke 6:38 TPT

Date

Giving It All Away

Yesterday, we talked about the prophetic and how you can use the gift God has given you of being able to hear from Him to help others. Today, as we get to the end of this journey together, our challenge to you is to think of what else you can take forward to include in your life. What else can you do, perhaps as a thank you to God, for the healing in your life that you've experienced as a result of your Sozo?

Here's a suggestion. Give it away.

What does that mean? Here are three of Bill Johnson's better-known quotes:

"You only get to keep what you give away."

"When you keep it within the walls, it dies. When you take it out where Jesus intended it to be, it happens."

"The Holy Spirit is imprisoned in the bodies of unbelieving believers."

Putting these three together, starting with the last, gives us an undeniable message. The Holy Spirit lives within you. If you keep Him just for yourself, you make Him a prisoner. His intention and Jesus' wish are for everyone to get out from behind our physical and mental walls and to tell others the Good News about Him. As we do so, we represent the kindness, generosity, and love of His nature. As we give ourselves in His service, we get back far more than we ever received. It's a great deal, isn't it? We give love, and we gain life!

Can you see that as we share our healing with others, we receive deeper levels of healing for ourselves? As we empty ourselves of all the lies, we fill ourselves with His truth, and then we give it away and get refilled with more of His truth. The extent of His truth and the depth of His love is never-ending. Enjoy the journey!

Reading:

> *Give generously and generous gifts will be given back to you, shaken down to make more room for more. Abundant gifts will pour out upon you with such an overflowing measure that it will run over the top! Your measurement of generosity becomes the measurement of your return.*
>
> Luke 6:38 TPT

Also Read:

Philippians 2:2

Hebrews 13:16

Prayer and Response:

> *Ask Father God what going and doing looks like for you. Where do you have influence? Where can you best represent Jesus in the market place of your daily life?*

Christ with me, Christ before me, Christ behind me,
Christ in me, Christ beneath me, Christ above me,
Christ on my right, Christ on my left,
Christ when I lie down, Christ when I sit down,
Christ in the heart of everyone who thinks of me,
Christ in the mouth of everyone who speaks of me,
Christ in the eye that sees me,
Christ in the ear that hears me.

Date

Reflection

How are you feeling? How has life changed? How has declaring the truths God told you during your Sozo helped to change your thinking and the way you do life? Has journaling every day helped to draw you nearer to God? If you feel like telling us, we'd love to know! Remember that inner healing is a never-ending process. Think of yourself as an onion with one layer after another being peeled off as you deal with the past and slowly get back to being what God created you as in the first place. There's always going to be more to do and more forgiveness to be done. That's not to discourage you. It's just to reassure you that if you're reading this and are aware of more issues cropping up, that's normal.

Don't stop now! Keep journaling! Keep that conversation and relationship with God going. He wants to hear from you in the good times as well as the bad. Don't give up if you feel you haven't arrived yet. Jesus never promised us a life without challenges. He just promised us the ability to overcome them. Keep worshipping… no matter what. Keep trusting and may Father God ever hold you in the palm of His hand.

Remember, you're unique. That's the way God made you. You are loved uniquely! You hear uniquely! You have a unique calling! And, you're very special!

Declaration:

This declaration is known as the prayer of St. Patrick, the patron saint of Ireland.

May it bless you.

I arise today
Through the strength of heaven;
Light of the sun,
Splendour of fire,
Speed of lightning,
Swiftness of the wind,
Depth of the sea,
Stability of the earth,
Firmness of the rock.
I arise today
Through God's strength to pilot me;
God's might to uphold me,
God's wisdom to guide me,
God's eye to look before me,
God's ear to hear me,
God's word to speak for me,
God's hand to guard me,

God's way to lie before me,
God's shield to protect me,
God's hosts to save me
Afar and near,
Alone or in a multitude.
Christ shield me today
Against wounding
Christ with me, Christ before me, Christ behind me,
Christ in me, Christ beneath me, Christ above me,
Christ on my right, Christ on my left,
Christ when I lie down, Christ when I sit down,
Christ in the heart of everyone who thinks of me,
Christ in the mouth of everyone who speaks of me,
Christ in the eye that sees me,
Christ in the ear that hears me.
I arise today
Through the mighty strength
Of the Lord of Creation.

Recommended Reading:

Sozo: Saved, Healed, Delivered by Dawna de Silva and Teresa Liebscher

Shifting Atmospheres by Dawna de Silva

How to Stop the Pain by Dr. James Richards

Culture of Honor by Danny Silk

Keep Your Love On by Danny Silk

The Importance of Forgiveness by John Arnott

Rejection by Steve Hepden

I Thought It Was Just Me (but it isn't): Telling the Truth About Perfectionism, Inadequacy, and Power by Brené Brown

The Gifts of Imperfection: Letting Go of Who We Think We Should Be and Embracing Who We Are by Brené Brown

Daring Greatly: How the Courage to Be Vulnerable Transforms the Way We Live, Love, Parent, and Lead by Brené Brown

The Homecoming by Jack Winter

Declarations by Steve Backlund

About the Author

Darrell lives close to Salisbury Plain in Wiltshire, England with his wife, Anthea. They have been part of the Sozo family since 2009 and lead the Sozo team at Bath City Church. They are Sozo facilitators and International Bethel Sozo Organisation trainers. Along with Liz Gregg, they are the originators of Sozo for Couples. Their purpose is to equip the equippers, and their passion is to see ever person walk into the fullness of their God given destiny.